Usborne

First Magic Painting
Dinosaurs

I'm a Pterodactyl!

I love munching leaves.
I'm an Ankylosaurus.

I'm a speedy Spinosaurus.

Watch out. I'm hunting! I'm an Allosaurus.

I'm big and slow.
I'm a Diplodocus.

I'm an Iguanodon with a swishy tail.

I'm a Plesiosaurus. I love to swim!

I'm a slow, strong Stegosaurus.

I'm a Dimorphodon.
Watch me soar!

Honk, honk! I'm a noisy Parasaurolophus.

I'm a Triceratops. Can you count my horns?

Usborne

First Magic Painting
Under the sea

I'm a starfish going for a walk

Hello! I'm an angelfish.

I'm a little crab
with clickety clackety claws.

See my spots and stripes?
I'm a clownfish.

Splash! I'm a sea turtle.

I'm a manta ray.
Look at my long tail.

I'm a beautiful butterflyfish.

I'm a seal.
Can you see my whiskers?

I'm a curly whirly seahorse.

I'm an octopus. Count my arms!

Careful of my spikes!
I'm a pufferfish.

I'm a hermit crab
with a swirly shell.

I'm a lionfish. Do you like my stripes and swirls?

Usborne

First Magic Painting
Zoo

I'm a terrific toucan.

Raaaar! I'm a splendid lion.

See me stroll!
I'm a slow tortoise.

I'm a sloth, just hanging around.

I love water!
I'm a hippo.

I'm a happy, playful tiger.

See my trunk? I'm an elephant.

Oo-oo! I'm a mischievous monkey.

See my spots? I'm a cheetah.

Hissssss! I'm a snake.